Cottages

Cottages

BRIAN D. COLEMAN
AND DOUGLAS KEISTER

Gibbs Smith, Publisher
TO ENRICH AND INSPIRE HUMANKIND
Salt Lake City | Charleston | Santa Fe | Santa Barbara

First Edition

11 10 09 08 07   5 4 3 2 1

Published by

Gibbs Smith, Publisher

P.O. Box 667

Layton, Utah 84041

Orders: 1.800.835.4993

www.gibbs-smith.com

Designed by Gabriella Hunter

Printed and bound in China

Library of Congress Cataloging-in-Publication Data

Coleman, Brian D.

  Cottages / Brian Coleman and Doug Keister. — 1st ed.

    p. cm.

  ISBN-13: 978-1-58685-897-1

  ISBN-10: 1-58685-897-1

  1. Cottages—Decoration—United States. I. Keister, Douglas. II. Title.

NK2195.C67C65 2007

747—dc22

                    2006103303

Acknowledgements

The authors wish to thank all of the homeowners and designers who graciously opened their homes to us, both of our Sandys (Mclean and Susanto), and as always, our fantastic agent, Julie Castiglia, and our wonderful editorial team at Gibbs Smith, Publisher.

Contents

Introduction

Just what is a cottage? Characterized as a small, romantic dwelling, a cottage can range from a simply restored fishing shack overlooking cattails on a riverbank to a colorful casita surrounded by cacti in a sunny southern Californian suburb. Casual, comfortable, and inviting, cottage interiors should not be too serious. They are a place to relax and unwind from the stress and pressures of modern life, an escape to a slower time and pace where simple pleasures can be appreciated.

Cottages gives ideas and inspiration from across North America for cottage-lovers of all persuasions. We take you to the picturesque Catskill Mountains in upstate New York, where rustic, nineteenth-century cottages perch on mountain slopes in charming communities with names like "Twilight." With interior staircases of golden birch logs, their bark still intact, and diamond-paned windows overlooking the treetops, these simple, mountain retreats are hard to resist. Furnished with warm, colorful Turkish rugs and pillows and simple tag-sale sofas and chairs, these snug cocoons are the perfect places to spend a long weekend just sipping hot chocolate and savoring the leafy tranquility of the mountaintop.

While many are rustic, cottages can certainly be urban as well—take, for example, a narrow aluminum and corrugated steel building that for all outward appearances is a small warehouse in an industrial area of Victoria, British Columbia. Once inside, you realize this is a futuristic creation—a true cottage of the twenty-first century, complete with furniture that slides away into the floor with the flick of a switch and an underground swimming pool.

The seashore is traditionally a favorite spot for cottages, and we visit a beautiful seaside community: sunny Tybee Island off the coast of southern Georgia. Full of small homes and diminutive guesthouses, many just plain wooden shacks built in the early twentieth century for summer and weekend holidays, Tybee Island today is a cottage lover's delight, thanks in a large part to designer and preservationist Jane Coslick. Over the past decade, Jane has restored dozens of these simple buildings, infusing them with new life and giving them a fresh, laid-back charm. Painted with bright, cheerful colors such as rain-slicker yellow and seafoam green and furnished in a casual country chic, these cottages invite you to take a deep breath, kick off your shoes, and just relax.

The appeal of cottages began for many in the 1920s with the resurgence of interest in historic architecture. Spanish Revival cottages in particular were appealing to homeowners, especially in California, where the climate and geography mirrors that of Spain. We visit a lovingly restored example in San Diego, whose red tile roof, rough plaster walls, and original wrought iron light fixtures evokes a simple and devout Franciscan monastery. Designed and built as a model home in 1926 by Richard S. Requa, a popular architect of the period, this cottage championed the simplicity of the sun-washed white stucco farmhouses of Spain.

Tom Mix was a popular star of the silent screen who spared no expense when he built a Spanish Revival cottage for his mistress in 1926 (even though she later left him to marry Hopalong Cassidy). Beautifully restored in the 1990s, the cottage features hand-stenciled ceilings, handsome Malibu tile fireplaces, and rooms painted in a colorful Mexican palette of bright blues, reds, and oranges. Furnished with period Mission, Spanish Revival, and Craftsman pieces, the cottage is at once colorful, comfortable, and inviting.

We hope that *Cottages* will help you to create a cottage of your own. Remember, a cottage can be anywhere—perched among trees on a mountaintop, nestled among the sand dunes on a sunny, windswept island, or just tucked away on a pleasant suburban lane. After all, it's really only a state of mind—a special spot to unwind and reenergize so that we can face life's challenges with renewed vim and vigor.

An Artist's Cottage

in the Catskills

*T*he Catskill Mountains in upstate New York have long been a favorite getaway for metropolitan New Yorkers, especially during summer when the heat and humidity of Manhattan becomes unbearable. Many resort communities were built in the area during the nineteenth century, including Twilight Park in 1887. Formerly sheep pastures, the development was perched on 160 steep acres of Round Top Mountain and offered unsurpassed views of the forested Kaaterskill Clove (Dutch for "canyon") below. Its founder, Charles F. Wingate, gleaned the community's name from New York City's Twilight Club, an organization of New York businessmen who met to discuss topics of general male interest (such as "How Should Our Girls Be Trained?"—a debate on the merits of women wearing corsets). Wingate was a tireless promoter, and it wasn't long before other members of the Twilight Club began discovering the Catskills' charms. They began purchasing lots and erecting rustic summer cabins. Over the next several decades, more than 100 cottages were built. While some were substantial, most remained simple and rural, with straightforward interiors of unstained wooden wainscoting and log stair railings, often golden birch with the bark still intact.

*Above: Joe likes to use the piano in the dining room as an easel to display some of his paintings. The great horned owl was a gift from a friend. **Opposite:** Constructed with split-log siding, the cottage is perched on the mountain slope and has sweeping views of the valley.*

When Joe Keiffer came across his Twilight cottage in 1989, it hadn't changed significantly since it was first built in 1897. Perched on a mountain slope, it seemed suspended in the surrounding trees, and balconies on three sides gave breathtaking views over the steep Clove below. Built for friends and followers of a local minister whose own house was just down the hill, the house was meant as a mountain retreat with split-log siding and interior walls of fir wainscoting. Nearly a century later, the old knob and tube wiring was still in use, the upstairs walls and woodwork had been painted an indigestible peppermint green, and the kitchen had been "modernized" in 1952 and (fortunately) never updated. But Joe, a professional artist, was drawn to the cottage's rustic charms and sweeping views that reminded him of a Thomas Cole painting. He set to work slowly restoring the home but keeping intact as much original detailing as possible. The parlor woodwork that had been painted white was methodically stripped and cleaned to restore its mellow glow. Joe also returned the simple brick fireplace to its original red brick. He revarnished the oak floors and cleaned and repaired the original sash windows to working order.

Joe used his artist's eye to guide him as he refurbished the rooms. Exotic influences were popular in the late nineteenth century (as seen in Olana, Frederick Church's Byzantine estate overlooking the Hudson River), so Joe added some exoticism of his own: a large, Oriental gong as a fireplace screen, colorful Chinese lanterns for lighting, and rows of peacock feather fans strung along the walls. Worn, comfortable wicker chairs, a Mennonite rocker from Pennsylvania, and enameled tin cups stacked on a shelf all helped create a casual, inviting ambience, one in harmony with the house and its humble nineteenth century origins.

The kitchen had not been altered since 1952, and Joe decided to honor its aesthetic (and follow the course of least resistance). He kept the plain wooden cabinets intact and simply cleaned and waxed the linoleum. A pea-soup green with butter yellow trim brightened the room. Joe found period appliances, including a gas stove with illuminated knobs and a "fabulous '50s" dinette set, and he strung colorful enameled pots and pans overhead for a soup-kitchen insouciance.

The gatehouse at the entrance to Twilight is appropriately adorned with the symbol for the community: an owl.

Bedrooms and bathrooms upstairs were kept basic, befitting a country cottage. Beadboard walls and ceilings were painted a restful white, and the bedrooms were simply furnished with brass beds and quilts. The two bathrooms still had their original fittings and these were carefully left untouched; even an early first aid box over the medicine cabinet was preserved.

Of course, a house is never finished, and Joe tries to tackle one major project each summer. Last year a retaining wall was rebuilt from hand-laid stones. The cottage and the Twilight community have become a source of inspiration for Joe, and he frequently paints scenes of the surrounding countryside. His realistic style paintings are now in demand in art galleries across the country. Simple, charming, and still inviting after over a century, this Twilight cottage remains what it was built to be—a relaxing mountainside retreat.

The rustic living room is centered on a brick fireplace. Note the beamed ceiling and wood paneling on the walls. Furnishings are an eclectic mix of tag-sale and antique shop finds, including exotic Chinese lanterns and peacock feather fans.

Above: Painterly piles of old, enameled tin cups fill bookshelves in the parlor.
Opposite: The dining room is centered on a nineteenth-century agricultural sorting table, a gift from Joe's parents. An early twentieth-century slag glass chandelier hangs overhead. Eleanor Roosevelt, a friend of the original owners, is said to have once dined in this room. The French doors are original and lead to the balcony.

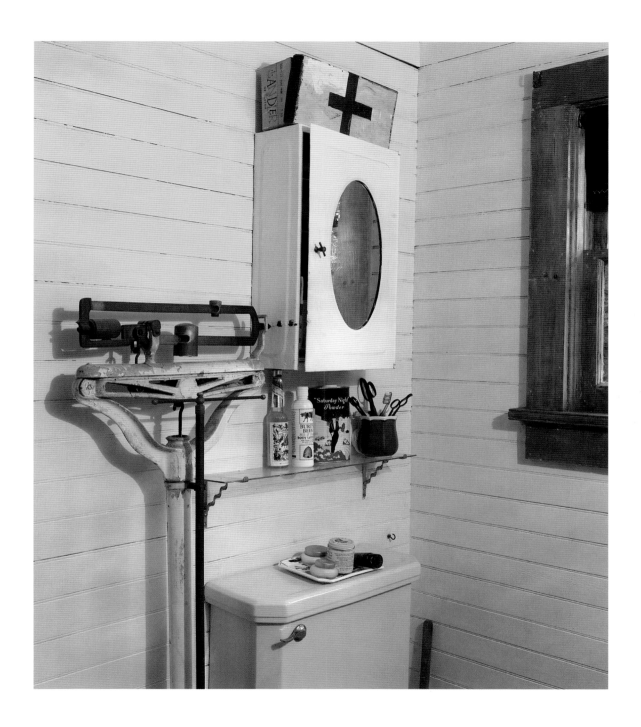

Above: The upstairs bathroom remains simple and contains the home's original first aid box. *Opposite:* A collection of vintage toilet bottles and tins makes a colorful display on a bathroom shelf.

Above: An original stained glass sidelight on the side of the front door lists the year of the cottage's construction: 1897.
Opposite: The master bedroom upstairs overlooks sweeping mountain vistas that stretch over thirty miles to the Berkshires in Massachusetts. A 1940s peeled cedar headboard fits with the rustic décor. The quilt was made as a wedding gift.

Color

in the Catskills

When Elena Patterson built her summer cottage in the Catskills, she initially painted it a simple, straightforward grey with white trim. But this artist and graphic designer, born and raised near Cape Town, South Africa, had grown up with the vibrant, invigorating colors of Africa. Inspired by San Francisco's "painted ladies," Elena decided to use a unique South African palette on her architecturally lacking cottage to add visual interest. Soon the main body of the house began to sing with Benjamin Moore's "Orange Blossom," "Jalapeno Pepper," and "Yellow Marigold," with bright lilac "Victorian Trim." It was hard to stop there—shutters were painted with interior scenes of the rooms, and in a moment of homesickness, Elena decided to bring the jungle to the Catskills and painted the front door with leopard spots.

*Above: Brilliant colors transformed this Catskill cottage and disguised its lack of architectural details. The shutters are painted with scenes of the interior rooms. **Opposite:** The leopard-spotted front door pays homage to the owner's South African roots. The striped ceiling adds visual impact and disguises the lack of architectural ornament.*

Elena's brilliant colors and sense of fantasy soon moved indoors as she transformed the home's ordinary rooms with color and whimsy. Using "unprecious" objects in unusual ways is a passion for Elena and so she designed everything from a floor lamp made of papier-mâché in the form of a woman to a chandelier enlivened with colorful South African beaded dolls. Collections of art are displayed on every surface. The periwinkle blue entry wall is covered with vintage letters of the alphabet, with a large gold "R" from a former Woolworth's sign taking center stage. A table covered with a Victorian hooked rug holds a menagerie of animals, including a lipstick-pink cat and banana-yellow giraffe made of recycled plastic bags. The adjacent dining room centers on a long glass table supported by carved teak dogs and human figures from Indonesia. Colorful South African candlesticks and green and red ostrich eggs decorate the tabletop. More art in the room includes two large carved panels of the Tree of Life and a Nigerian taguna post from an Uruba tribal meetinghouse.

The living room is just as vibrant. Periwinkle blue walls display collections of African tribal masks and green and yellow Majolica plates. An overstuffed chair was too staid, Elena decided, so she painted a more pleasing brown over its cowhide design. Glass bowls of orange and yellow paper flowers, low carved and beaded African Zulu stools, and an Indian daybed used as a coffee table give the room an exotic and delightful appeal.

The upstairs master bedroom is a great room in which to wake up—rich "Raspberry Mousse" pink paint adorns the walls, and the sloping ceiling is painted a contrasting "Copper Penny" orange. Himba African baskets hang above the headboard, and Moroccan bed coverings echo the room's parfait colors. In an ode to the medieval fortresses of Morocco, decorative metallic nail heads cover a wardrobe on one side. Color invaded a son's bathroom as well. Covered in blue Mexican tiles, the room is accented with red and white, including a vintage Coca-Cola sign and a whimsical beaded elephant from Monkeybiz South Africa.

Periwinkle blue walls and a multi-hued door and woodwork make the entry into a fantasy. Old advertising-sign letters are arranged on the wall. The beaded Queen's chair is from South Africa.

It wasn't long before people began talking about the unusual house up the road in Tannersville. Elena found sightseers outside in all weather and at all hours. With a spirit of the community in mind, she approached the mayor of Tannersville and suggested painting some of the town's nondescript buildings in her joyful African palette to attract tourists and revitalize the small township's sagging economy. Now her Paint Project has become a reality. The block-long downtown is emerging like a butterfly from its cocoon, and interest is growing with coverage from television shows, national newspapers, and magazines. Color, it turns out, can transform not only cottages but a whole town as well.

The living room overlooks the yard and is a riot of color, with periwinkle blue walls and accents of primary colors. More African art, including masks and plates, are hung on the wall. African stools rest in front of the fireplace.

Above: A carved wooden dog and human figures from Indonesia help support the glass-topped dining table. The chandelier was dressed up with handmade beaded African dolls from Monkeybiz South Africa, a nonprofit organization for disadvantaged women in Cape Town that has revived the art of handmade beadwork. Colorful collections of art include carved teak tree-of-life panels flanking the window and a rare taguna *meetinghouse post on the far left.* **Opposite:** *A standing floor lamp, nicknamed "Lamp Oile," was made in papier-mâché by the owner and was the star of a New York art exhibition.*

Above and right: The master bedroom is sunny and bright with a parfait of colors: ragged "Raspberry Mousse" walls and a "Copper Penny" ceiling. African baskets hang above the bed. Cheerful throw pillows in tangerine, citrus, and lime green add to the tropical color palette.

Opposite: Inspired by Moroccan fortresses, the wardrobe was designed with rows of decorative nail heads on the doors. A pink Moroccan pile rug rests on the floor. Above: A son's bathroom is colorfully tiled in bright blue Mexican ceramic tiles with a vintage red Coca-Cola tin sign and a comfortable wicker chair.

Witchwood

Cottage in Upstate New York

Onteora, a resort community in upstate New York begun in 1888 by the famous artist Candace Wheeler, has many charming and picturesque cottages. One of these, Witchwood, was built in 1890 for Mrs. Mary Knight Wood, who was a well-known composer and musician. (Her song "Ashes of Roses" was played at the 1892 Chicago Exposition.) Originally just a modest cabin centered on an open, two-story parlor, Witchwood's location was breathtaking, perched near the top of the mountain with sweeping views of the surrounding Catskills. Mrs. Wood was active in the arts and she left her creative touch throughout the house: bold musical notes were painted on the stone mantels above the fireplaces and guests were invited to sketch mementoes of their stays on the stair risers—a permanent registry of the artistic and talented visitors.

Time was not kind to Witchwood, however, and by the time the current owners purchased it several years ago, the house had become a "hodge podge lodge." Interior woodwork had been painted a hospital green, the original porch railings had decayed and fallen off, and the exterior resembled a Peter Max painting with Band-Aid pink siding and green trim. The two-story living room stone fireplace was leaning thirty degrees and pulling down the foundation of the house, and every window and door needed removal and restoration. The owners, however, were not deterred—they called in Iliana Moore, a designer and longtime Onteora resident whose own home exemplified the potential charm of a properly restored and refurbished Onteora cottage.

Above: Ornate strapwork hinges decorate this exterior door, which was painted the original exterior red. *Opposite:* The great room is centered on a two-story granite fireplace. Burlap and fir paneling cover the walls and a nineteenth-century Oriental rug helps anchor the room.

Iliana used period photographs to help in the restoration and to provide details that were no longer present. The exterior was returned to its original wood shingles with red windows, doors, and trim. The foundation was restored, the parlor stone fireplace was straightened and repointed, and soon musical notes danced above the crackling fireplace once again. Original burlap was replaced on the walls and Mrs. Wood's artistic guests' drawings on the risers were cleaned and preserved. Bathrooms were updated and period fixtures preserved, including the original claw-foot tub. Furnished with warm Turkish rugs and throws and comfortable furniture, Witchwood was finally returned to the special and creative retreat it was a century ago.

*Above: Guests including Elizabeth Bacon Custer (General Custer's widow) wrote mementoes of their visits on the stair risers. The mementoes have been carefully preserved. **Right:** The library is centered on a stone fireplace and furnished with rustic chairs and stools.*

 Opposite: The master bathroom still has its original claw-foot tub and is furnished with late-nineteenth-century antiques, including a jelly cupboard and a
child's horse and toys. *Above:* Mrs. Wood originally had musical notes painted on
the mantels in honor of her talents as a well-known composer and musician.

Opposite: An upstairs guest bedroom is paneled in knotty pine bead board and has a secluded sleeping alcove above. A vintage Suzani cloth covers the brass bed.
Above: A rustic log ladder just big enough for an adventuresome child leads to a tiny sleeping alcove above. A nineteenth-century painted wall shelf and old prints decorate the wall.

Columbine

Cottage in the Catskills

In the nineteenth century, women led a far different life than they do today. The "fair sex" was not allowed to vote or own property, and it was even considered "improper" for women to hold full-time employment. Candace Wheeler, one of the most influential artists of the period, was a champion for women's rights and self-sufficiency. She helped organize many projects, including a summer retreat in 1888 that she created for her friends and named "Onteora," a local Indian name. Accessible by train, it was just a five-hour journey from New York City, and it wasn't long before Onteora became well known as an artist's sanctuary. Mark Twain was a frequent visitor, as was Mary Mapes Dodge, editor of *St. Nicholas Magazine*. Other visitors included General Custer's widow, Elizabeth Bacon Custer, and Maude Adams, J. M. Barrie's friend and the first Peter Pan. About 120 homes were built on the forested, 1,600-acre mountaintop site over the next twenty years, all in a rustic, vernacular style. Surprisingly little changed over the next century, and while most were only used as summer cottages and some fell into disrepair, many survived nonetheless.

*Above: A 1903 Onteora fair poster and paper fans from the Chicago 1893 World's Fair are displayed on the mantel. **Opposite:** The exterior of the house was painted black with red trim for a rustic nineteenth-century appeal.*

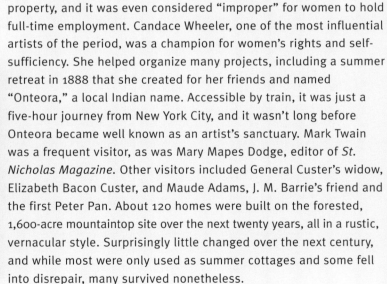

One of Candace Wheeler's frequent guests was Ruth McEnery Stuart, a well-known author of the time (Mark Twain used to call the trio of Onteora women—Candace Wheeler, Ruth McEnery Stuart, and Elizabeth Custer—"the old cats"). In 1902, using the proceeds from her books, Stuart bought Columbine Cottage, a comfortable summer retreat built in 1891 and named after the local wildflower. Two stories tall, the home featured fir wainscoting, wooden beamed ceilings, a large brick fireplace in the living room, and a broad front porch affording views of the leafy forests beyond. When Iliana Moore's parents bought Columbine Cottage in 1969, it had not yet been modernized and extensive updating was required—new plumbing, heating, and electrical systems were installed and the house was winterized for year-round use. Iliana, a professional designer, grew up in the house and continues to enjoy it today with her family. She has freshened and updated the interiors, but in a sympathetic manner, making sure to keep the home's rustic charm intact.

The living room is the center of the house and is comfortably furnished with kilim-covered furniture. Original fir bead board wainscoting and ceilings were carefully kept intact.

Iliana painted the dining room a warm, Pompeian orange and covered the windows with colorful linen drapes that feature fruit, reminiscent of the many apple trees in Onteora, which still produce bountiful crops each summer. Iliana collected examples of Ruth McEnery Stuart's works, and she enjoys displaying the books and sheet music on the dining room buffet. A local furniture company made the dining table and chairs, which are original to the house. (In fact, many of the cottages in Onteora are still furnished with their early-twentieth-century products.) The living room, the center of the house, is warmed by a large brick fireplace that displays Onteora memorabilia, including a poster for the 1903 local fair (Onteora sponsored an arts and crafts fair each summer) and paper fans from the 1893 Chicago World's Fair. Simple, comfortable furniture, including a pair of Thebes stools, kilim-covered furniture and pillows, and a flat-weave Oriental rug, make the room at once warm and welcoming. Original details to the house such as the golden birch stair railings and the bead board ceiling were all carefully preserved. Upstairs, the master bedroom is filled with a four-poster canopy bed, along with bookshelves and an original side table. Vintage textiles, including an antique tablecloth above the bed and an Irish linen skirt on the dressing table, lend to the casual and inviting appeal, making this home one that Iliana hopes to continue enjoying for many years to come.

*Above: Ruth McEnery Stuart memorabilia are displayed on the dining room buffet, along with apples from local trees. Brown and white nineteenth-century transferware is displayed on a plate rack above. **Opposite:** The dining room was enlivened with warm Pompeian orange walls and a c. 1890 stained glass chandelier. The dining table and chairs are original to the house.*

*Opposite: These rustic stair railings were made from golden birch logs with the bark still intact. The caned chair is Egyptian Revival, c. 1880. **Above:** Family hand-me-downs and flea market finds were used throughout the house; here a lampshade made from sea shells, a vintage Paisley table throw, a Victorian silver egg cup stand, and a stack of old books are invitingly grouped together on a living room side table.*

The master bedroom is centered on a four-poster bed hung with an antique table-cloth. The bookshelves and drop leaf table are original to the house. **Opposite:** *A skirted table in the corner displays a Bakelite vanity set, c. 1930, which belonged to the owner's mother.*

Space Age

Cottage in Canada

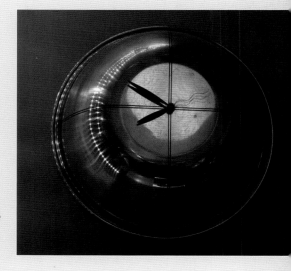

*V*ictoria, British Columbia, nestled on the southern tip of Vancouver Island in Puget Sound, is a traditional and very English city. Named for Queen Victoria, its winding streets are lined with tidy bungalows and comfortable cottages with manicured yards and brightly colored flowers. It's something of a surprise to find Shahn Torontow's home built on a former parking lot in the city's industrial district. For all outward appearances a plain, steel warehouse, the narrow building is just ten feet wide, thirty-five feet long, and twenty-four feet tall. But once you step inside, you realize this is no ordinary building—it's a true urban cottage built for the future, fit for the Jetsons and Space Age living.

*Opposite: Sited in an industrial neighborhood, the vertical metal siding and mirrored windows make the structure seem more like a commercial building than a private home. **Above:** An aluminum pan is recycled into a wall clock in the kitchen.*

Shahn, a talented furniture builder and designer, opted to erect his urban cottage on a small lot in an unlikely location after zoning restrictions prevented him from building a mixed-use residential and commercial building. He soon became a trendsetter, as four additional residences have now been constructed in the neighborhood. Shahn used commercial materials throughout in homage to the site, constructing the exterior with a siding of ribbed galvanized steel. The long and narrow interior rooms are nonetheless open and airy and are accessed by a central, open steel staircase, which winds around an elevator shaft (initially a fire pole was installed, but it was replaced by the more practical lift). Shahn was not deterred by the minimal amount of space. He went underground in the small backyard, adding a subterranean swimming pool, accessed by a concealed staircase beneath the patio that rises with the flick of a switch.

Shahn's inventiveness is evident throughout. The home's whimsical furnishings include "Media Momma," a large robot-like holder for media equipment, and a master bed that slides away into a recess in the floor when not in use. Ceilings are ribbed galvanized steel decking. Industrial materials are even carried into the kitchen, where aluminum floor treading was used for the kitchen cabinets and counters were lined in stainless steel. Bright color accents, including fire engine red on the stairs and fuchsia pink for the railings, bounce off the shiny metal surfaces and give the home an energy and sparkle that is both welcoming and unique. A spaceship that looks ready to blast off, this unique urban cottage is a tribute to the imagination and creativity of its designer. 🏠

From the entry deck across to the kitchen, the use of commercial products continues with cabinets of aluminum floor treads, exposed metal ductwork, steel decking on the ceiling, and halogen lighting that is motion activated. Bright colors soften the space and make it more welcoming.

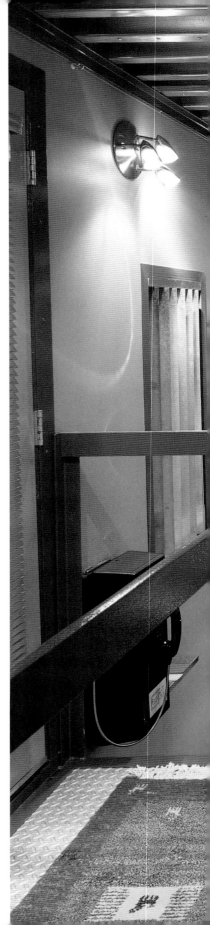

Above: Aluminum floor plates have been made into storage cabinets in the entry.
Opposite: Polished aluminum tread plates are used as cabinet doors in the kitchen.
A stainless steel backsplash and halogen lights add to the futuristic look.

Opposite: In the second-floor living room, hand–rubbed fir floors are contrasted against curved galvanized steel wall panels. A "Media Momma" robot designed by the owner holds television and stereo equipment at the rear of the room. *Above:* A neon porch light above the front door beckons with an iridescent, atomic glow.

Above: A stainless steel surface–mounted basin in the bathroom reflects the light of the corrugated, galvanized aluminum backsplash. **Opposite:** *The slate-covered, poured concrete underground pool is maintained at a constant temperature of 90 degrees using radiant heat. It is accessed by a recessed stairway that rises up to ground level with the flick of a switch.*

*Left: The master suite features a queen bed that automatically retracts into the floor when not in use. The halogen lighting is motion activated. **Above:** Locally made ceramic fish heads decorate the wall above a soaking hot tub in the corner of the master bedroom.*

Time Out

on Tybee Island

$\mathcal{T}$ybee Island, a five-mile-long barrier island just off the coast of southern Georgia, has had a long and interesting past. "Tybee" means "salt" to the Euchee Native Americans, the original inhabitants of the island who found abundant supplies of the mineral there. When the Spanish arrived in 1520, they soon realized that the oat grass and sand dunes were good not only for salt but also for sassafras root, a valuable and popular remedy at the time. Pirates, too, discovered the island and found that it made a good hideaway to stash their stolen treasures. Tybee's location at the mouth of the Savannah River made it strategically important; it played important roles in the country's defense from the Revolutionary War to World War II. Following the Civil War, the island became a resort area for nearby Savannah, its cooling breezes a welcome relief from the summer heat and humidity of the city. By the 1890s there were more than 400 beach cottages and buildings for the summer residents, and for many years Tybee remained a popular getaway. But by the 1990s the island had become all but forgotten. Developers began eyeing the tiny ocean cottages and simple beachfront fishing shacks for condominium developments. Fortunately that is also when Jane Coslick, who would end up saving many of these properties, moved there and bought her first cottage in 1993.

A hammock on the porch is the perfect spot for an afternoon siesta.

Jane, an interior designer and passionate preservationist, had recently become an empty nester and was looking for an escape, a healing place where she could permanently be "out of town," breathe fresh ocean air through open windows, and walk barefoot on the beach. The little cottage with the For Sale sign just fit the bill. Built in the 1920s, the 625-square-foot home had been erected as temporary housing for the Army Corps of Engineers while they built the first road to Tybee (before then it had only been accessible by boat or train from Savannah). Previous owners, however, had not paid much attention to the little structure. Low seven-foot ceilings of plywood had been nailed over the original wooden ceilings and were covered with black mold. Everything inside, from floor to ceiling, was painted in beige. The kitchen was an unappetizing blend of orange countertops and dark brown cabinets; even the original heart pine floors had been covered with dark brown paint. But the location was perfect: set behind a sand dune on a quiet cul de sac and cleverly named "Ninety-Nine Steps from the Beach," this was exactly what Jane had in mind. She began by tearing out the plywood ceilings to expose the rafters overhead. (She had to get rid of the snakes nesting there first.) French doors were installed to bring light into the room, and Jane scoured the local salvage yard for vintage hardware and trim. The heart pine floors were refinished and walls painted a fresh white with nautical periwinkle blue trim to make the small rooms seem larger. A kitchen island was added, and a rack for wine glasses made from an old window frame was hung overhead from newel posts, which were turned upside down and attached to the vaulted wooden ceiling. Jane's entire family was enlisted in the restoration—her son Bauer painted the tiny bathroom with waves and her sister Patricia Walton added fish and crabs, making it a simple pleasure to wash one's face in the tiny sink. With a hammock hanging on the screened sun porch, this was Jane's perfect retreat, one with happiness and joy radiating from every nook and cranny.

A screened porch wraps around the front of the cottage and lets in the ocean breeze.
Jane added a small deck on the roof to watch ships in the nearby harbor.

Opposite: A small room off the porch was made into a guest bedroom, the exterior windows left unchanged to accent the cottage's makeshift charm. Above: A cheerful yellow and white wicker settee on the front porch is the perfect spot for sipping a glass of lemonade and watching the world go by.

Opposite: Simple blue and white striped slipcovers were used to cover the furniture found at local tag sales and salvage stores. *Above:* "Dress casual"—after all it's just a beach house! An old blue tin watering can makes an amusing lamp.

Above: The small original bathroom was given a touch of whimsy and humor with hand-painted waves, fish, and crabs. *Opposite:* A heart pine breakfast bar separates the living room from the galley kitchen. The rack for cups and glasses was made from an old window frame.

Above: Found furniture in the bedroom was given a wash of white paint to keep it clean and simple, just as life at the beach should be. ***Opposite:*** Wainscoting and wooden shutters on the interior windows were painted white in the bedroom to expand the space. The closet doors beside the bed are merely decorative.

Luscious

Little Cottage on Tybee

Once Jane Coslick had restored her first cottage on Tybee Island, it wasn't long before she began noticing others in need of restoration. One day while walking her dog, she noticed a tiny, derelict, one-room shack built in the 1920s that was now slated for demolition. The owner wanted to build a new log home on the lot, and after Jane was unable to convince him to save the sad structure, she ended up buying it for $1 and moved it to a vacant lot next to her home. She named it "Luscious Little Cottage" to prove those wrong who said it was not salvageable or worth saving. The 300-square-foot house was given a new lease on life with nine pocket windows for light and breeze, an outdoor shower, and a tiny but light-filled bedroom alcove which was created with a half wall divider. White was used liberally on the walls and ceiling to expand the space, and accents of cheerful color were added: turquoise, pink, yellow, and blue. Jane placed a large, soft daybed right by the front door for lounging and watching the ships pass through Savannah Harbor. She couldn't pass on a salvaged ticket booth, which she moved to the rear of the property and turned into an extra sleeping porch (named "The Roost," it has beds made from found driftwood). Now rented, Jane appropriately advertises the cottage as a home for "Authentic Cottage People."

The tiny one-room cottage was a derelict shack before Jane rescued it and moved it next to her house.

Top: *The small bed alcove was created with a half wall divider, keeping it light and open.* **Above:** *A lobster wall sconce in the bed alcove is quite appropriate for a seaside cottage.* **Left:** *The one room is divided into a small kitchen, bedroom, and lounge for watching ships pass by in the harbor. Bright accents of color keep the white room cheerful and inviting.*

Above: The former ticket booth, which Jane named "the Roost," was converted into a sleeping porch with beds made from local driftwood. *Opposite:* A salvaged ticket booth was moved to the back yard and converted into extra sleeping quarters. Note the outdoor shower on the right, perfect for washing off sandy feet after a walk on the beach.

Tybee Shutters

When Jane Coslick, Tybee Island's resident preservationist, got a call that several sets of original, burnt peanut red, five-foot tall shutters were being discarded from a cottage "restoration," she didn't hesitate for a moment. While she couldn't save the sixty-five-year-old cottage from being remuddled, she was able to rescue its striking shutters. With simple tree cutouts, the shingles were just what she needed for her current restoration project. In fact, Jane made the shutters into the home's logo, using them everywhere she could—at the front gate, as doors for the outdoor shower, even as headboards in the bedrooms for the rustic appeal of camping out.

*Above: Bright turquoise blues are reflected in the original crusty paint preserved on these shutters. **Opposite:** Rescued 1940s shutters were recycled into everything from the front gates to the outdoor shower door (far left). Quite appropriately, the cottage was named Tybee Shutters.*

Jane restored the small structures (originally a cottage and adjoining apartment), carefully preserving original detailing, and joined them together to create a comfortable, 1,200-square–foot, family-friendly retreat. A large covered front porch was designed with colorful red-and-white-striped fabrics as a haven from the heat of the summer; it also doubles as extra sleeping space for overnight guests as well as for those essential midday naps. Jane kept the rooms bright and airy, painting the original bead board walls a simple white and adding colorful accents from flea market forays (including a growing collection of paint-by-number art, which hangs in the hallway). Casual and laid-back, Tybee has quickly become a favorite escape for the cottage's owners from the pressures of the office. After all, isn't that what a cottage is all about—bike riding and swimming, kayaking and collecting sea shells, watching the sun rise and set from a hammock on the porch? And, Jane reminds us, there's no better place to take time out than on Tybee.

A wide, screened sleeping porch is cool even on the warmest of summer days and is the perfect spot for a peaceful nap.

The family enjoys watching videos and eating popcorn here in the evenings. Vintage white enamelware accessories lend a period appeal to the newly added kitchen.

Opposite: Jane Coslick used weathered shutters for the headboard of her bed in her own Horsepen Creek cottage. A vintage animal print fabric was used for pillow shams. Surround yourself with the things you love, she advises—thus, a bird's nest brimming with eggs rests on the table. *Above:* Fabulous '50s flamingoes decorate the daughters' room, which also includes more paint-by-number artwork on the walls.

Above: Paint-by-numbers art found at local flea markets lines the long hallway and adds a tropical touch. *Opposite:* The shutters were used as headboards in the master bedroom, their original burnt peanut red color carefully preserved.

Palm Cottage

on Tybee Island

"You're nuts!" Jane Coslick remembers the Tybee City marshal laughing when she informed him she was buying this derelict cottage and restoring it. Certainly the 600-square-foot structure had seen better days. Built for the Army Corps of Engineers in the 1920s, it had serious dry rot and was missing essential features—including a bathroom and a front door. But Jane was determined to prove her doubters wrong. After buying the cottage for $1 and moving it to a new lot (as the land it stood on was being sold), she enlisted the help of her contractor friends and with astute planning turned the former ugly duckling into a sparkling two-bedroom and two-bath showpiece. Jane carefully preserved as many of the original features as she could, from pocket windows in what was once a porch (now a guest room) to the twelve-inch corner sink in the powder room, which was expanded into a second bath with the addition of an outside shower. Interior wood-work was recycled from a nearby 1920s apartment building that had been demolished. French doors were added to the screened porch, now an additional living space and the perfect spot for reading the paper and sipping afternoon tea. Painted "Beach Glass" blue with bright yellow and turquoise accents, the cottage is now a star and has been featured in national magazines—copies of which even the city marshal has on his desk. 🏠

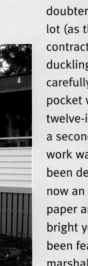

*Above: The unpretentious cottage sparkles with bright colors and whimsical accents, including shutters with palm tree cutouts. **Opposite:** The owner loves to iron linen shirts and towels to relax, so Jane included a fold-down cottage-size ironing board overlooking the backyard.*

The screened porch is an additional living
space used for craft projects, reading, and
afternoon tea.

Above: The view from the main room into the bedroom reveals refinished and restored heart pine floors, as well as walls reconstructed from salvaged woodwork from a nearby demolished apartment building. Colors were kept simple and cheerful to enlarge the space. *Right:* The main room of the cottage is divided by a tin breakfast bar into a kitchen/eating space and a sitting area. Open shelves help keep the room simple and visually expand the walls.

Above: Part of the front porch was enclosed to make a guest room. Jane carefully preserved the pocket windows to add light and character. **Opposite:** Pocket windows and recycled siding were painted basic white to expand the small guest room and keep it fresh and inviting.

Cottage Color

on Tybee Island

$\mathfrak{J}$t's easy to spot Jane Coslick cottages on Tybee Island. Color, boldly applied from top to bottom, is what makes them stand out; they sing with bright rain slicker yellows, ocean wave aquas, and rich fire engine reds—colors that make people smile and relax, which is, after all, what living in a cottage is all about.

This small cottage built in the 1940s was slated for demolition, but Jane was able to save it from the wrecking ball and move it to its present site, a shady lot next door to Palm Cottage, another of her colorful creations. Later, poorly built additions were removed and the home's good "bones" were restored, preserving details such as two-over-two windows, interior bead board siding, and a raised dining room (originally a sleeping porch). The walls were kept simple and white, and accents of colors chosen from a fabulous '50s palette inspired by the owners' vintage-style kitchen china—Princess Grace turquoise, seafoam green, chartreuse, and fiery red. The bright colors were carried outside to the exterior with a sunflower yellow body accented in turquoise and mango red. Cottages, Jane reminds us, are powerfully emotional dwellings and should reflect love and happiness inside and out.

Once slated for the wrecking ball, this 1940s cottage was rescued and moved to a shady lot on Tybee Island. Cheerful colors were chosen to make the cottage sing: sunny yellow with turquoise and mango red accents.

An eclectic assortment of comfortable furnishings was used in the living room; the raised dining room (originally a sleeping porch) is separated by interior shutters from the rest of the cottage.

Above: The bedroom is simple and inviting with white bead board walls and an old painted brass bed. *Opposite:* Turquoise was carried through to the bathroom to help tie the small rooms together.

Opposite: A '50s dinette set found at a local thrift store was the perfect fit for the retro-style kitchen (and is probably similar to what was used originally). The cabinet doors on the left conceal modern necessities: a washer and dryer. *Above:* An amusing sign in the kitchen sums up the Tybee Island cottage philosophy.

Tybee

Fish Camp Cottage

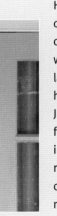

Jane Coslick had passed by the abandoned fish camp cottage on Tybee Island many times while walking her dog, but had never paid it much attention. But when it came onto the market she realized that the sorrowful 1940s shack needed saving. With views across the back toward Horse Pen Creek, it would have been a prime target for a developer to tear down in order to build a new house or condominium. The weather-beaten cottage certainly had its share of problems: the front porch had rotted off, windows were warped and stuck open, and the tiny garage wasn't even large enough for a modern vehicle. Serious rot was everywhere—the roof had caved in and the refrigerator had fallen through the kitchen floor. But Jane was not put off. She began by collecting a couple of her carpenter friends and attaching the garage to the house with a breezeway, making it into a master bedroom. Original bead board walls and ceilings were restored and brightened with a coat of fresh white paint. Jane brought the outside in by using accents of color inspired by flowers in the yard— morning glory blue, sunny yellow forsythia, soft pink Lady Bank roses.

*Above: A hand-painted sign reminds visitors of the definition of "cottage." **Opposite:** The exterior of Fish Camp Cottage was painted a cheerful morning glory blue inspired by a favorite blouse. The garage on the right was attached to the house and made into a master bedroom.*

Unattractive jalousies were replaced with standard double-hung sashes to help let more light into the rooms. A tin roof (which lasts forever and is especially romantic in the rain) replaced the rotted original, and the kitchen was brightened with a backsplash of yellow, white, and blue Mexican tiles Jane found for fifty cents a piece. A cheerful new yellow and white checkerboard floor and bright blue cabinets were added to coordinate with the tiles. To bring back some curb appeal, she found a favorite blue blouse in her closet, had the paint store match the color (it's now called "Favorite Blouse Blue"), and then painted the cottage with it. Shutters with star cutouts were added for a touch of whimsy. And, of course, Jane was not finished once she had restored and sold Fish Camp Cottage—she turned around and bought the house behind it to preserve the marsh views and rescue yet another vintage Tybee cottage.

*Opposite: The enclosed front porch was made into extra living space and connected with a pass-through into the kitchen. **Above:** Original cabinets were freshened with bright colors—blue with white and red accents.*

Above: A breezeway was added to connect the former garage—now the master bedroom—to the main house. The small passage now doubles as a study. *Right:* Found objects and simple furniture painted white make the house both unpretentious and charming.

Calypso

Cottage on Tybee

Built in the 1940s, Calypso Cottage is the home of Becky and Jim Heflin, who own www.tybeecottages.com, a rental agency for cottages on the island. With the expert guidance of designer Jane Coslick, the cottage was brought back to life with amusing and colorful fabrics and furnishings, accented with local art. Color is everywhere in the dining room, from enticing red drapery panels accented with green polka dots (the curtain rods above are painted passionate purple) to a bright green, red, and yellow painting by Blanche Nettles hanging on the wall. The living room is a mixture of cheerful yellow walls decorated with sunwashed paintings of Tybee. And even the grandchildren's bedroom is awash in color with robin's egg blue walls and a rain-slicker-yellow adjoining bath. The Heflins, with the help of Jane Coslick, have certainly captured Caribbean essence, color, and charm in their colorful island cottage.

*Opposite: Calypso Cottage, built in the 1940s, was restored with splashes of Caribbean color—hot pinks, yellows, and blues. **Above:** A colorful painting by local artist Blanche Nettles Powers (who exhibits her work at her Rosewood Studio in Savannah) hangs on the wall.*

The dining room was given new life with yellow walls, bright red drapery panels, and red and green accents, such as the lime green ruffle on the dining table bench. The bright red French doors open to the pool. Local artists made the lively, whimsical art in the room.

Above: The living room is painted in a sunny yellow and furniture is slipcovered in comfortable, easily maintained fabrics for the beach. *Opposite:* The grand-children's room is cheerful with bright blue walls and a rain-slicker-yellow adjoining bath.

Amazing Grace

on Tybee Island

"*A*mazing Grace"—the hymn that celebrates being once lost but now found again—is an apt name for this Tybee Island cottage and the story of its rescue in 2003. Built in 1904 for Captain George Walker, the cottage was part of a turn-of-the-century real estate development called "Colony Row" on Tybee Island's Back River. The large, comfortable cottages featured one- and one-half-acre lots, two stories, and wraparound porches with beautiful views and boardwalk access to the beach. Servant quarters and bath houses were built at the back of each house.

The 1904 beach house features wraparound porches and was painted a soft, sandy gray. The former servant quarters on the left were converted to a guesthouse.

When the current owners, a young couple with three children, came across the cottage for sale, they knew they would only purchase it if they could have it restored by Jane Coslick, Tybee Island's most well-known preservationist who had already rescued more than a dozen cottages scattered around the island. And the house did need restoring—acoustic tile ceilings and faux wood paneling had been applied over the original bead board walls and ceilings, and unattractive aluminum windows had replaced double-hung wooden sashes that had once let the ocean light stream in. The porch as well as many of the rooms had rotting boards. Jane immediately agreed to restore the cottage and save an important part of Tybee Island history, while also making it livable and bringing it into the twenty-first century.

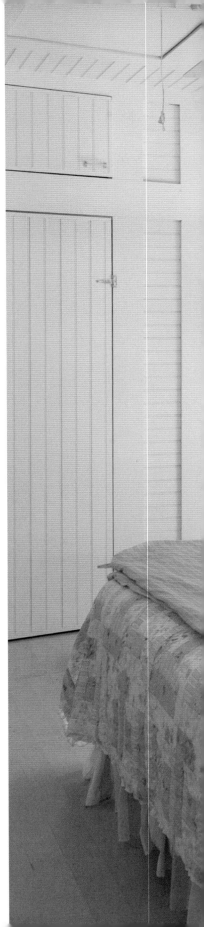

Above: A group of vintage milk glass compotes rests on a bedside table in the master suite and is lit by a glass lamp with a simple lace-covered shade.
Right: The guest suite is light and airy with white walls and an aqua blue floor. Artwork over the bed reinforces the pastel colors.

Jane and her carpenter, Bruce McNall, replaced rotten woodwork, saving as much of the original as possible. They removed the offensive acoustic tiles and imitation wood paneling. Rooms were opened up to create airy and light-filled spaces looking out to the sand dunes and beach. The original pine floors were refinished, and a cottage-style kitchen was created from a former bedroom and shower, with cabinets reaching to the ceiling and a white farmhouse style porcelain sink. Bunk beds were added for the children and the former servants' out-building was carefully conserved and converted into a sunny guesthouse. Jane used a beachcomber's palette for the house, washing the walls and ceilings in sunlight white but using colors of the sea as accents—soft aquas, blues, and gray-greens. The exterior was painted a special color created by Jane called "Tybee gray," a softly weathered, sandy seaside gray. The homeowner loves to collect antiques and immediately began filling the house with the spoils of her treasure hunts—painted wooden benches and old church pews, colorful McCoy pottery, collections of school globes, and Victorian tins and enamelware. Relaxing, inviting, and comfortable for the whole family, this beachside cottage has truly been graced with love and a new lease on life.

Left: Flea market finds such as Victorian enamelware, tin signs, and a weathered pie safe in the corner add instant patina and character to the downstairs kitchen. Above: Collectibles in the kitchen include everything from birdhouses and scales to a Tybee Island advertising sign dating from the '40s.

Above: *One of the children's bedrooms is kept fun and colorful with pillows made from vintage quilts and old painted and weathered furniture.* ***Opposite:*** *Bunk beds with a top railing designed as a miniature picket fence were built in one of the children's bedrooms. Casual painted furniture keeps the room simple and inviting.*

The sunlight-filled master bath centers on a long claw-foot tub perfect for soaking while gazing out at the beach. Sea-inspired colors were used—white with accents of soft blues and greens.

Spanish Revival

Simplicity in San Diego

What is it about a Spanish Revival cottage that is so appealing? For many, it's the inherent simplicity of the style, reminiscent of sixteenth-century Franciscan monasteries with red tile roofs, roughly hewn stucco and plaster walls, Moorish archways, and wrought iron fixtures. It's a rustic charm of Andalusian farmhouses of northern Spain with central courtyards added for outdoor living. Southern California is much like Spain in both climate and geography, and by the 1920s many architects in the area were building in the popular style, including Richard S. Requa, who constructed this picturesque cottage in 1926 as a model home for his practice.

Above: The white stucco exterior and red tiled roof were purposefully kept plain and unadorned to suggest a simple Spanish farmhouse. **Opposite:** *A carved wooden ecclesiastical chair and a Spanish Revival wooden table set an appropriate tone in the small entry hall.*

Purchased in 1983 by retired publicist and historian Parker H. Jackson, the home had been a rental for many years and thus, fortunately, was never significantly altered. Parker found the original wrought iron wall sconces, simple casement windows, even the fancy chimney top (a replica of a Spanish farmhouse chimney top Requa photographed during his travels there) untouched. He freshened the white stucco walls (keeping them white, as Requa recommended, to reflect the sun and keep the house cool), replaced worn floorboards with oak, and enclosed the loggia, opening it up to the center of the home. Using period photographs, Parker found Spanish Revival furnishings which would have been used in the home, a 1920s wrought iron fire screen, a tooled leather chair, even photographs of Requa himself and Requa's wife and son, which Parker hung on the dining room wall. Requa's Spanish Revival cottage once again beckons with the tranquil simplicity of a Spanish monastery, cool and inviting in the southern Californian sun.

Above: The small arched fireplace was meant to resemble a country farmhouse fireplace; the homeowner accented it with a period wrought-iron fire screen found in Mexico. *Opposite:* Generous glazed casement windows let light stream into the long living room, which is accented with a faux box-beamed ceiling. The wall sconces are original. Furnishings are a combination of family antiques and finds from local antique shops.

Sponsored by the Monolith Cement Company, Requa traveled to Spain in 1926 and 1928 and published these portfolios of his trips.

Above: A brass 1920s Spanish Revival floor lamp and tooled leather chair in the living room are similar to the original furnishings. *Opposite:* The dining room opens to the formerly open loggia, now an enclosed passageway to the kitchen and bedrooms. The carved walnut buffet holds family silver and china.

Above: An arched window in the dining room overlooks a courtyard filled with pots of lush tropical plants in keeping with Requa's recommendations. *Opposite:* The farmhouse kitchen looks out to the courtyard and holds an early twentieth-century coal and wood-burning stove. The table was hand carved in 1940 in Puerto Rico for the owner's father who was stationed there. The c. 1925 wrought iron chandelier was found at a neighborhood tag sale.

Casa Paloma

in Pasadena

When Michael Llewellyn and his partner, Tom Rotella, first saw the 1926 Spanish Colonial Revival cottage for sale in Pasadena, California, they knew right away it was anything but ordinary. The house was originally built in Brentwood as a secret gift from silent screen star Tom Mix to his mistress Dorothy Sebastian, a George White's Scandals showgirl who became a movie actress and later married another cowboy—film legend William Boyd (a.k.a. Hopalong Cassidy). During her heyday, Dorothy entertained costars such as Joan Crawford and Anita Page here. But by 1987, the once-charming but now unwanted and outdated cottage faced demolition. Fortunately, its owners recognized its provenance and decided instead to donate it to Cal State. The school dismantled and stored it until 1991, when artists Michael and Rennie Rau Marquez purchased the historic home and moved it to its present site, a sunny lot on a palm-lined boulevard in Pasadena. They spent over a year meticulously restoring the house, returning the elaborately stenciled living room and coffered dining room ceilings to their original splendor and replacing modern reproduction chandeliers and wall sconces with period-appropriate pieces. The original fireplace, with stenciling and handsome Malibu tiles, was cleaned and put back into working order. The stucco exterior was painted a pleasing golden peach. Interior rooms were given new life in a bright Mexican palette of primary blues, yellows, and oranges inspired by Frida Kahlo's Casa Azul in Mexico City. The Marquezes designed and planted the cactus and succulent gardens around the home and were in fact awarded a Pasadena Golden Arrow Design Award in 1993 for their outstanding work.

The 1926 classic Spanish Revival cottage in southern California was relocated, restored, and landscaped with drought-tolerant plants native to the area.

Luckily when Michael and Tom bought the home in 2004, only minor cosmetic work was needed. They refined the gardens by adding focal points of statuary, graveling dirt paths (which had turned to mud during winter rains), and putting out pots of seasonal color. Interior work involved little more than repainting a bedroom and decorating with an eclectic blend of period Mission, Craftsman, and Santa Fe furnishings found everywhere from local antique shops and flea markets to trips to nearby Mexico. The owners have a penchant for ecclesiastical art; *santos* (Mexican religious carvings) and Greek Orthodox altar doors, coronas, crosses, and *retablos* grace the walls and are grouped on tables throughout the house. Just under 1,800 square feet, this historic casita has been given a second lease on life and once again is a colorful, comfortable, and much-enjoyed cottage.

The living room, like the house itself, is a comfortable amalgam of Old Mexican, Spanish Colonial and Revival, California Rancho, Native American, Mission, and Traditional styles. The Cowboy Room beyond is decorated with a mural of Tom Mix shooting early cowboy films in the desert.

*Above: Hand-stenciled ceilings in the living room were restored and accented with a period 1920s wrought-iron chandelier. **Opposite:** The original front door's Spanish ambience is enhanced with an ornamental tile font and lantern.*

*Opposite: Oaxacan folk art keeps company with rare 1920s California Mission pottery bookends and a 1930s St. Martin figurine on a library table in the living room. Henry, the owners' dachshund, sits in his favorite chair in the corner. Note the hand-stenciled tiles around the fireplace. **Above:** Artist Michael Marquez's mural of Monument Valley in the Cowboy Room pays homage to early moviemaking and the house's first owner. Mission-style chairs enhance the Old West ambience.*

Above: In the Cowboy Room, photos and movie posters from the 1920s include silent screen star Dorothy Sebastian (center left), original owner of Casa Paloma. Paramour and cowboy film star Tom Mix (lower right) gave the cottage to Dorothy, who later married another Western movie legend, William Boyd (center right), better known as Hopalong Cassidy. *Opposite:* A c. 1890 Santa Fe blanket chest supports altar panels celebrating the Annunciation from an early twentieth-century Greek Orthodox Church. Other objects displayed on the table include two nineteenth-century Mexican ceremonial crosses, a silver art nouveau box, and a brass corona from a santo.

*Opposite: A pair of 1930s Mexican ceramic corn jars complements a dinette set from the same period in the sunny yellow breakfast room. **Above:** Bold stenciling on the ceiling was added to complement the hand-stenciled beams original to the cheerful breakfast room. The tin chandelier is from Mexico.*

The colors of the kitchen were inspired by
Frida Kahlo's Casa Azul. Vintage pottery
includes a Fiestaware pitcher and a set of
1950s souvenir California Mission glasses
in the foreground. An antique Mexican
angel stands guard over the adjoining
breakfast room, whose walls are painted
with a mural of the Day of the Dead, a
Mexican holiday.

Above: An antique carved and hand-painted wooden santos, *or saint, from Mexico keeps guard on a sideboard.* **Opposite:** *Original parquet floors and a stenciled and coffered ceiling grace the dining room, which is filled with folk art, colorful pottery, and religious artifacts.*

Above: Folk art and paintings are displayed in the master bath, which is painted in pastel lilac and creams—a quiet departure from the bright colors used elsewhere in the cottage. **Opposite:** In the guest bedroom, a 1920s English barley twist bed is paired with an African campaign chair, a vintage serape, and artwork from Mexico and Peru for a colorful, eclectic appeal. The house was split down the rear hallway before being moved from Brentwood to Pasadena; bright stenciling conceals the reassembly point.